The Cypress Said Hello To Me

© Monique Hardman 2024

The rights of Monique Hardman to be identified as the author of this work have been asserted by her in accordance with the Copyright, Designs and Patents Act of 1988.

All rights reserved; no part of this publication may be reproduced, stored in a retrieval system, or transmitted in any form or by any means, electronic, mechanical, photocopying, recording or otherwise without the prior written consent of the publisher or a licence permitting copying in the UK issued by the Copyright Licensing Agency Ltd. www.cla.co.uk

ISBN 978-1-78792-067-5

Book design, layout and production management by Into Print
www.intoprint.net
+44 (0)1604 832149

MONIQUE HARDMAN

The Cypress Said Hello To Me

Dedicated in her loving memory,
Michele Oganesian.
Spreading her love and kindness
forever and always.

With love,
Your flower

As I walk along the sea
the cypress says hello to me.
Her arms reach over and above,
that shades me from the warmth and sun.
Step by step, I hear it creak,
the wooden path beneath my feet.
And as the tunnel reaches near,
the sounds of nature become clear.
That sometimes all you need for peace,
is the sound of the boardwalk
on Moonstone Beach.

Its rays melted through my skin
and as the warmth traveled through me
I realized, that life is the purest gift of all.

My body begins to ache,
like limbs of a tree
on a dark winter's night.
I look to the pine with
her needle like leaves,
which have helped her adapt
to retain more seeds.
And as I carry life's adversities,
I find my strength in nature
that I did not see.

And as she floats up in the sky,
she spreads her light throughout the night.
Not shining for praise like the sun,
just bringing peace to those she loves.

Cotton candy skies,
swirls of pink and blue.
You can almost taste the hue
that brought me back to you.

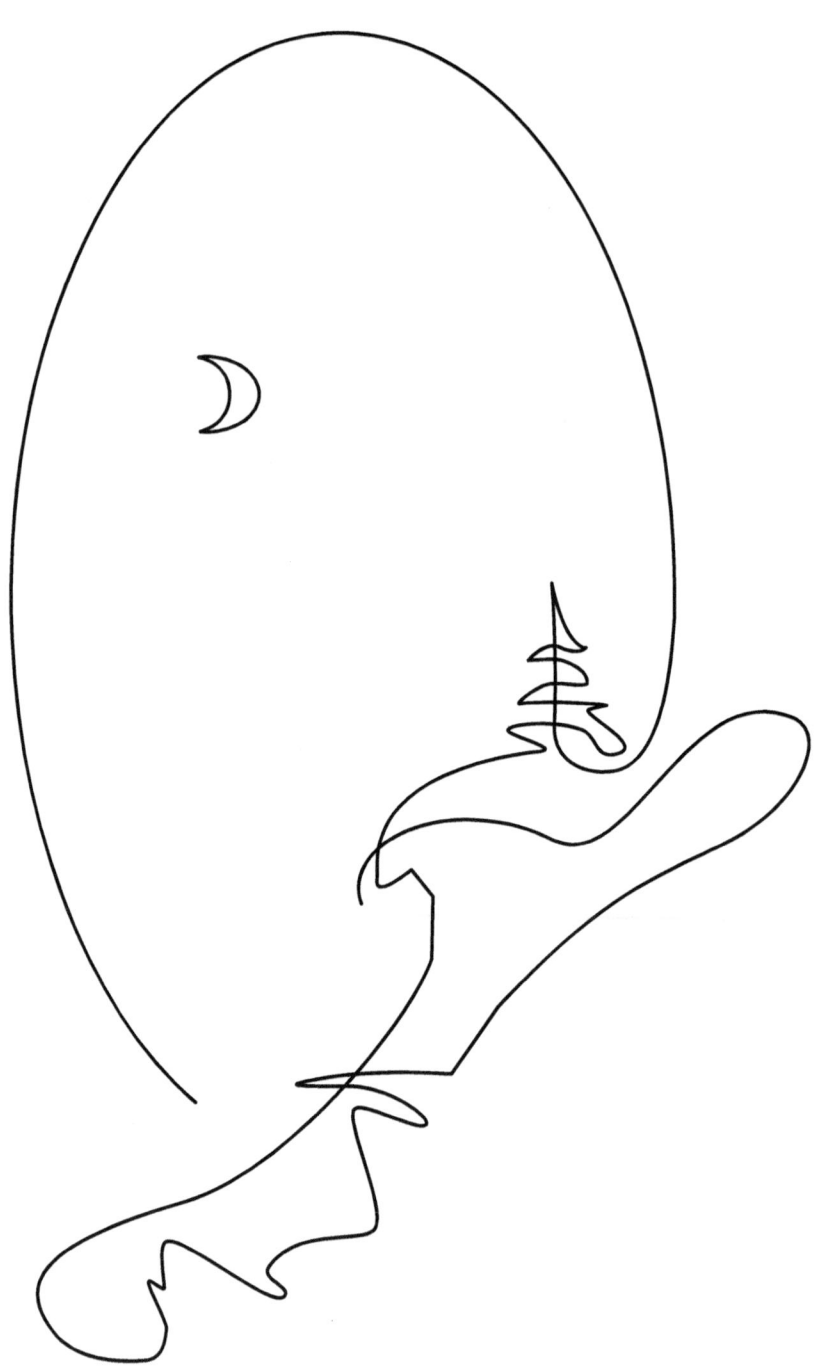

And as you go about your day
I hope you don't forget,
that when the blue sky fades to grey
your dreams are not at rest.

And with each season
not only comes beauty,
but a lesson to be learned.
When it becomes cold and dark,
and the rain settles in,
a vibrant future is ahead.
A colorful view filled with life.
And when the heat seems to drain us
of all that we can bear,
a cool midnight sky is near.
And when the trees start to dwindle,
and the leaves begin to fall,
we realize that change can be
the greatest gift of all.

The way you stay connected
to her roots below.
You water and love her,
without others needing to know.
Your humble and gentle ways
as you make her shine,
creating a garden that is truly divine.

In a world full of breathtaking color,
we are still learning to love a shade
other than our own.

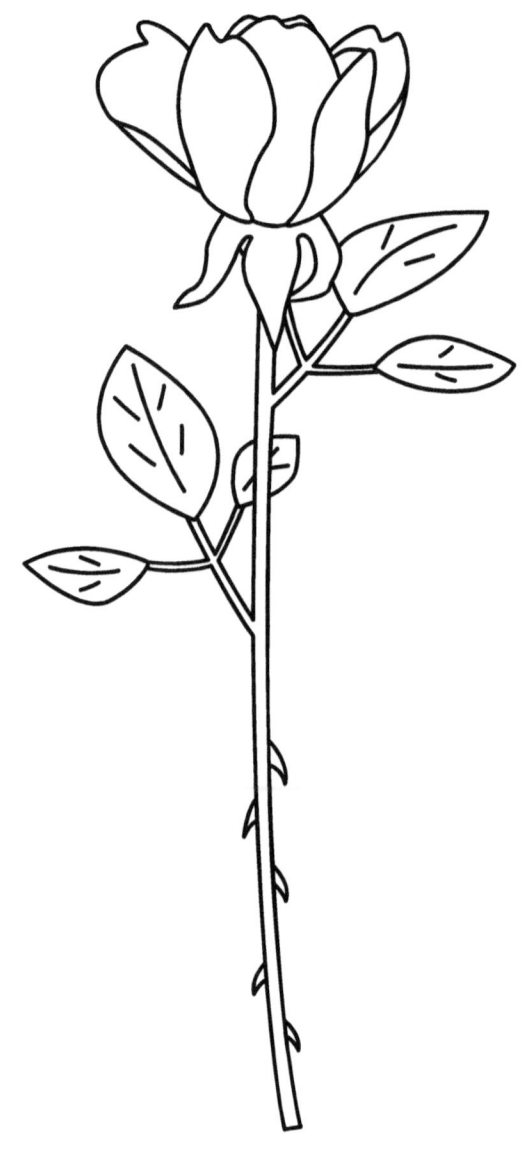

Love for another does not die,
it is recreated into something beautiful.
Through pastels, movement, and melody
it colors and dances its way
back into life.

When it's hard for you
to find your way,
I'll open a new path.
When you can't see
the beauty that I see,
I'll show you your reflection
smiling back at me.
When doubt creeps in,
I will remind you
of all you have achieved.
For your friendship is
the greatest gift
God has given me.

And when the sun
kissed the sky,
yellow and blue
would fade to night.
Your star dancing
in a stream,
as it lulled me
back to sleep.

The tides washed over me
with memories of you.
They cleansed and calmed
my weary mind.
Sun's warmth wrapped all around me
with hugs long overdue.
For this is where we use to meet
laughter, love, and play.
I often look for you here
to relive my favorite day.

Her imagination
ran more freely
than she did,
but she never stopped
chasing the impossible.
With hopes of one day
catching up to them.

For He is shaping me
and building you up.
So that one day
when we meet,
our foundation will withstand
the test of time.

His hands were solid gold
melting all over her.
Worth more than diamonds
and stronger than steel.
She could not put a price
on his love.

The living drift to sleep,
to escape reality.
Hoping to be awakened
by their dreams.

For her heart
knew no boundaries.
She loved with all her being;
as she danced along the edge
without fear of the unknown.

How does one describe
the different shades of green,
that dance against the sunlight's rays.
Or the wind that sways the trees
to the raven's song,
as the pair serenade one another
to their beck and call.
A hue of golden fields
that have no end.
Mother nature is an art,
that must be heaven-sent.

We often look for meaning,
in our ordinary day.
But maybe the purpose of life
is to simply live,
until we can no longer stay.

www.ingramcontent.com/pod-product-compliance
Lightning Source LLC
Chambersburg PA
CBHW041929040426
42444CB00018B/3469